HarperCollins*Publishers*

First published in 2011
by HarperCollins*Publishers (New Zealand) Limited*
PO Box 1, Shortland Street, Auckland 1140

Copyright © Natalie Oldfield 2011
Food styling by Michelle Burrell
Thanks to The Haven, Devonport, and Babushka Antiques, Westmere
for their generous loan of props.

HarperCollins*Publishers*
31 View Road, Glenfield, Auckland 0627, New Zealand
25 Ryde Road, Pymble, Sydney, NSW 2073, Australia
A 53, Sector 57, Noida, UP, India
77–85 Fulham Palace Road, London, W6 8JB, United Kingdom
2 Bloor Street East, 20th floor, Toronto, Ontario M4W 1A8, Canada
10 East 53rd Street, New York, NY 10022, USA

National Library of New Zealand Cataloguing-in-Publication Data
Oldfield, Natalie.
Gran's family table / Natalie Oldfield.
Includes index.
ISBN 978-1-86950-910-1
1. Cooking. I. Booker, Dulcie May, 1913-2009. II. Title.
641.5—dc 22

Cover design and typesetting by Gas Project
Internal photographs by Todd Eyre
Colour reproduction by Graphic Print Group, South Australia

Printed in China by RR Donnelley on 140gsm Woodfree

Recipes inspired by Dulcie May Booker

GRAN'S FAMILY TABLE

NATALIE OLDFIELD

HarperCollins*Publishers*

CONTENTS

INTRODUCTION

Food, family and love ... these three things have become intrinsically linked and intertwined with who I am and what I value in life. They are for me the very essence of where I came from, and where I continue to travel.

My wonderful grandmother, Dulcie May Booker, is once again the inspiration for this book, just as she was for my first book, *Gran's Kitchen*. Although Dulcie has now passed away, our family will always admire the way she lived her life. So it is with her in mind that I have written *Gran's Family Table*.

This book is quintessentially about creating moments of joy, happiness and celebration through the preparation, sharing and eating of food.

This book is about the meals we share with family and friends. It is about honouring the past and shaping the future. It is about generosity, love, nourishment of the soul, and embracing the pleasures of preparing and cooking flavoursome food. This book is quintessentially about creating moments of joy, happiness and celebration through the preparation, sharing and eating of food.

For this book I have again drawn recipes from Gran's collection, and I've also included additional recipes from my mother Heather. My sister Michelle and I have also included our own family favourites, sometimes adding our own personal touches and variations.

Most of the recipes I have included are tried and true and originate from the family tables of past generations. As I share these recipes with you, I hope the richness of past memories shared will inspire you to create your own memories, as you sit at the table with those you love.

I have dedicated each chapter to each mealtime, beginning with breakfast, lunch and dinner. I have also included a chapter for puddings, as there was seldom a meal at my Gran and Pop's or my parents' home that didn't conclude with a deliciously decadent dessert. Also included are: salads and sides, providing the finishing touches to your family table; and preserves and dressings, the perfect gifts for friends and family.

Many of us lead busy lives, and although we live differently from the generations before us, let's not deny ourselves the simple pleasures of meals shared and memories created.

It has been such a pleasure spending time reading through Gran's old recipe compendiums again while putting this book together. Before Gran passed away, I asked her to go through her cookbooks and circle her most favourite recipes for inclusion in this book. These recipes encapsulate her style of cooking — all centred around simple, fresh and flavoursome food. So, with this in mind, I have endeavoured to provide meal options that are delicious, rich in flavour and colour, and easy to cook. Many of us lead busy lives, and although we live differently from the generations before us, let's not deny ourselves the simple pleasures of meals shared and memories created.

One of the many things I admired about my Gran was her ability to be adventurous with food, as well as the exuberant way in which she expressed her enjoyment when tasting new recipes and flavours. Gran never lost this vibrancy of spirit, and, even at the age of 96, she maintained an interest in trying new things, such as pesto, which she especially loved — things she would never have made in her heyday.

Home is where the heart is, and I believe that food created from the heart is, or should be, the centre of the home environment.

Home is where the heart is, and I believe that food created from the heart is, or should be, the centre of the home environment. I hope this book inspires you to cook delicious, simple food, gather your dearest ones around your own table, and share the love with them.

NATALIE OLDFIELD

BREAKFAST

Sharing breakfast with family or friends is a treat. It's an opportunity to celebrate the beginning of a new day with delicious food and warm conversation. I have many wonderful childhood memories of such breakfasts with my Gran and Pop. As children, my sister and brother and I would often stay at our grandparents' for the night. The next morning, as the sun rose above the countryside of Weymouth, we'd scurry into Gran and Pop's room and jump into bed with them. Somehow we all managed to squeeze into their double bed, cuddling, laughing, and talking excitedly about what we would have for breakfast. Whether it was a steaming bowl of porridge with brown sugar that soaked into pools of fresh cream; scrambled eggs with tangy tomatoes; or thick slices of hot buttered toast with Gran's apricot jam — we were never disappointed.

Gran would spread her morning table with all kinds of sumptuous delights. There was always more than one option to choose from, as she took great pleasure in seeing those she loved nurtured and fed.

These childhood memories will linger with us forever, as they have become woven into the very fabric of our lives. I will always remember the creating and sharing of those breakfasts as a magical way to begin the day.

BREAKFAST

BREAKFAST FRUIT AND NUT CRUMBLE

380 g can sliced apples
425 g can sliced pears, drained
4 tbsp maple syrup
2 tsp vanilla essence
1 tsp ground cinnamon
¼ tsp freshly ground nutmeg

Crumble
1 cup flour
½ cup brown sugar
½ cup rolled oats
½ cup crushed round wine biscuits
¼ cup shelled pistachio nuts, chopped
¼ cup walnuts, chopped
¼ cup sliced almonds
100 g melted butter, cooled to room temperature

Preheat oven to 160°C.
Place fruit, maple syrup, vanilla essence, cinnamon and nutmeg in a saucepan and simmer over a gentle heat for 10 minutes. Remove from heat and keep warm.
Mix crumble ingredients together in a bowl. Sprinkle evenly on an oven tray and bake for 20–30 minutes, or until golden brown.
Place warm fruit mixture into breakfast bowls and sprinkle with crumble mix. Serve with Greek yoghurt.

Serves 4–6

CRUMPETS

300 ml milk
300 ml water
2 tsp sugar
1 tsp salt
7 g active dried yeast
450 g plain flour

Warm milk and water together. Place all ingredients in a mixer with
a dough hook and beat for 2 minutes until smooth. Alternatively, mix
thoroughly with a wooden spoon until smooth. Set bowl aside until
mixture is frothy and doubled in size, about 20 minutes.
Grease and heat a heavy-based frying-pan to a medium heat. Using
a greased 9-cm ring, half fill with mixture and cook for 6–7 minutes
until it starts to bubble. Reduce heat until bubbles burst. Turn
crumpets over and cook for a further 2 minutes.
Repeat process until mixture is all used.

Makes 8–10

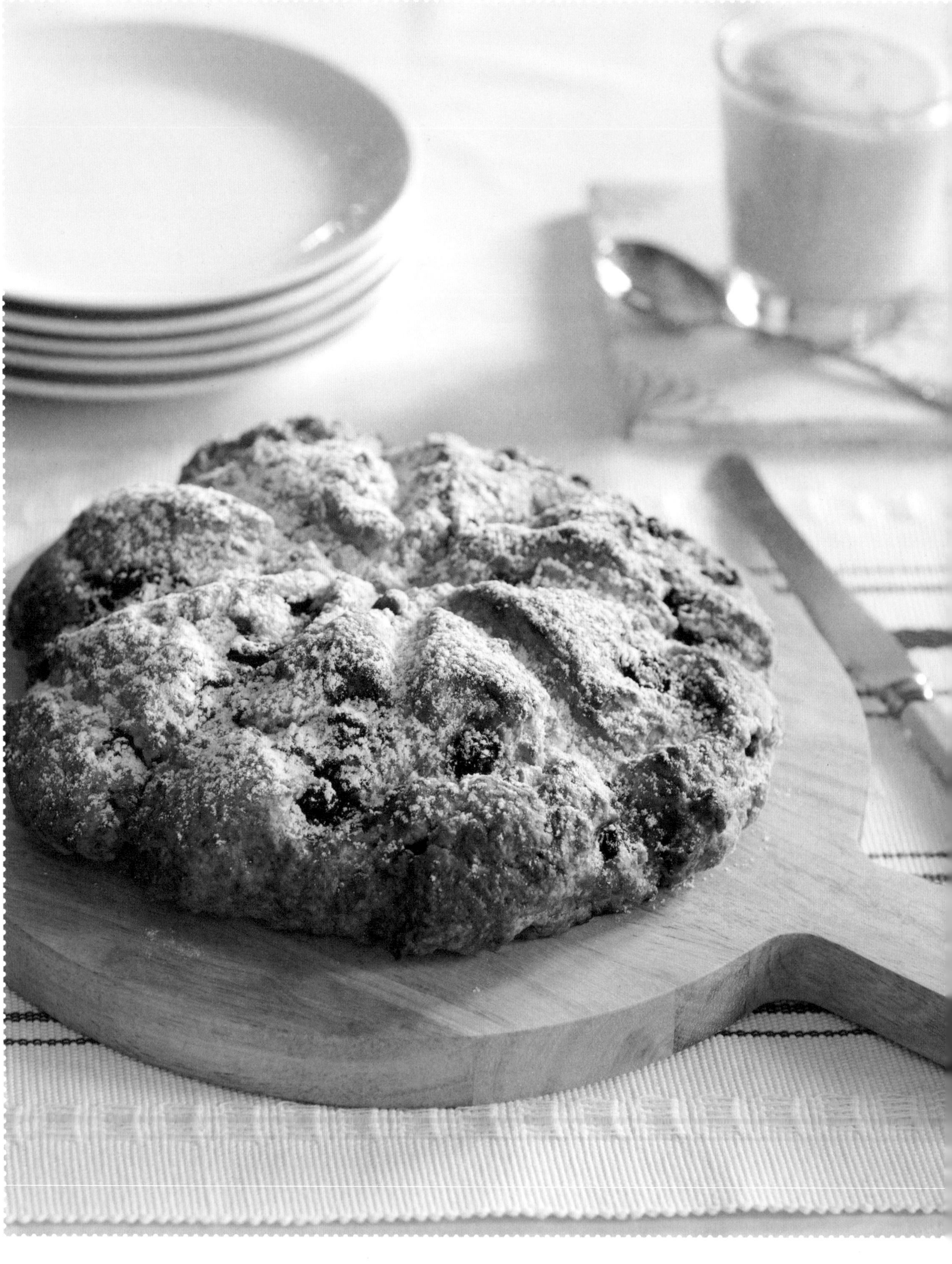

BIG BLUEBERRY BREAKFAST SCONES WITH LEMON CURD

1 ⅔ cup self-raising flour
2 tbsp sugar
100 g cold butter, chopped
½ cup cream
2 eggs, lightly beaten
¾ cup blueberries
a little milk for brushing
lemon curd, see p. 22

Preheat oven to 200°C.
Place flour, sugar and butter in a food processor and pulse until combined (but with a few small lumps of butter throughout).
Tip into a bowl and gently stir in cream and eggs, then fold through blueberries.
Turn mixture out onto a lightly floured bench and press into a 15-cm circle. Cut into 8 wedges, place on lined baking tray, brush with milk and bake for 20–25 minutes until golden and crunchy.
Serve with lemon curd.

Serves 8

LEMON CURD

zest of 2 lemons
100 ml lemon juice
100 g caster sugar
2 eggs
2 egg yolks
90 g butter, cut into cubes

Place all ingredients in a heavy-based saucepan, leaving out half
the butter. Cook over a medium heat and whisk continuously.
Once mixture reaches boiling point, continue to whisk for a further
1 minute.
Remove from heat, add remaining butter and stir until melted.
Cover the surface with plastic food wrap and allow to cool to room
temperature before serving.
Excess can be kept in the fridge in a jar with a tight-fitting lid for
up to 3–4 weeks.

Makes approximately 1¹/₂–2 cups

GRILLED BANANAS ON BRIOCHE WITH YOGHURT AND HONEY

2 ripe bananas
2 tbsp honey
2 thick slices brioche, toasted
1 cup Greek yoghurt

Preheat grill to 200°C. Peel and slice the bananas lengthways. Place the halves in a foil-lined baking pan and drizzle with 1 tablespoon of honey. Place under hot grill for 2 minutes or until golden brown. Place on top of brioche and spoon over yoghurt and remaining honey.

Serves 2

GRILLED GRAPEFRUIT WITH MAPLE SYRUP AND CINNAMON

2 grapefruit, halved
4 tbsp soft butter
½ cup maple syrup
¼ tsp cinnamon
4 tbsp golden raisins

Preheat grill to 220°C.
Leaving grapefruit halves in their skins, carefully slice through grapefruit segments to separate them. Mix together butter, maple syrup and cinnamon.
Place grapefruit on a foil-lined baking tray. Spoon over maple syrup mixture. Grill for 4–5 minutes. Sprinkle over raisins and serve hot.

Serves 4

SPELT BREAD

4 cups white spelt flour
2 cups brown spelt flour
2 cups warm water
2 tsp active dried yeast
3½ tbsp sunflower oil
2 tbsp honey
½ tsp salt
1 tbsp xanthan gum (optional)

Preheat oven to 180°C. Grease 1 large or 2 small loaf tins.
Combine white spelt flour and brown spelt flour.
In a mixer with a dough hook combine water, yeast, oil, honey,
salt, xanthan gum (if using) and half the flour mix. Mix on low speed
until smooth. Alternatively, mix thoroughly with a wooden spoon
until smooth.
Add remaining flour, 1 cup at a time, while mixer is still running.
Once all flour is mixed through, increase speed to medium and mix
for about 5 minutes.
Turn dough onto floured surface and shape into a large loaf-tin size,
or two small loaf tins. Place dough in prepared tin, or tins, cover and
leave to rise in a warm place until doubled in size. Uncover and bake
for 30–35 minutes for 1 large tin, 20–25 minutes for 2 smaller tins,
or until golden brown on top.
Remove from tin immediately and cool on a wire rack.

TASTY EGGS

1 tbsp lemon juice
½ tsp cumin
½ tsp smoked paprika
1 tbsp olive oil
4 eggs
1 tbsp mint, finely chopped
salt and pepper

Combine lemon juice, cumin and smoked paprika.
Heat oil in frying-pan over a medium heat.
Crack eggs carefully into the hot oil.
Spoon over spice mixture, then sprinkle chopped mint
evenly over each egg.
Cook to your liking and serve with toast. Season with salt
and pepper.

Serves 4

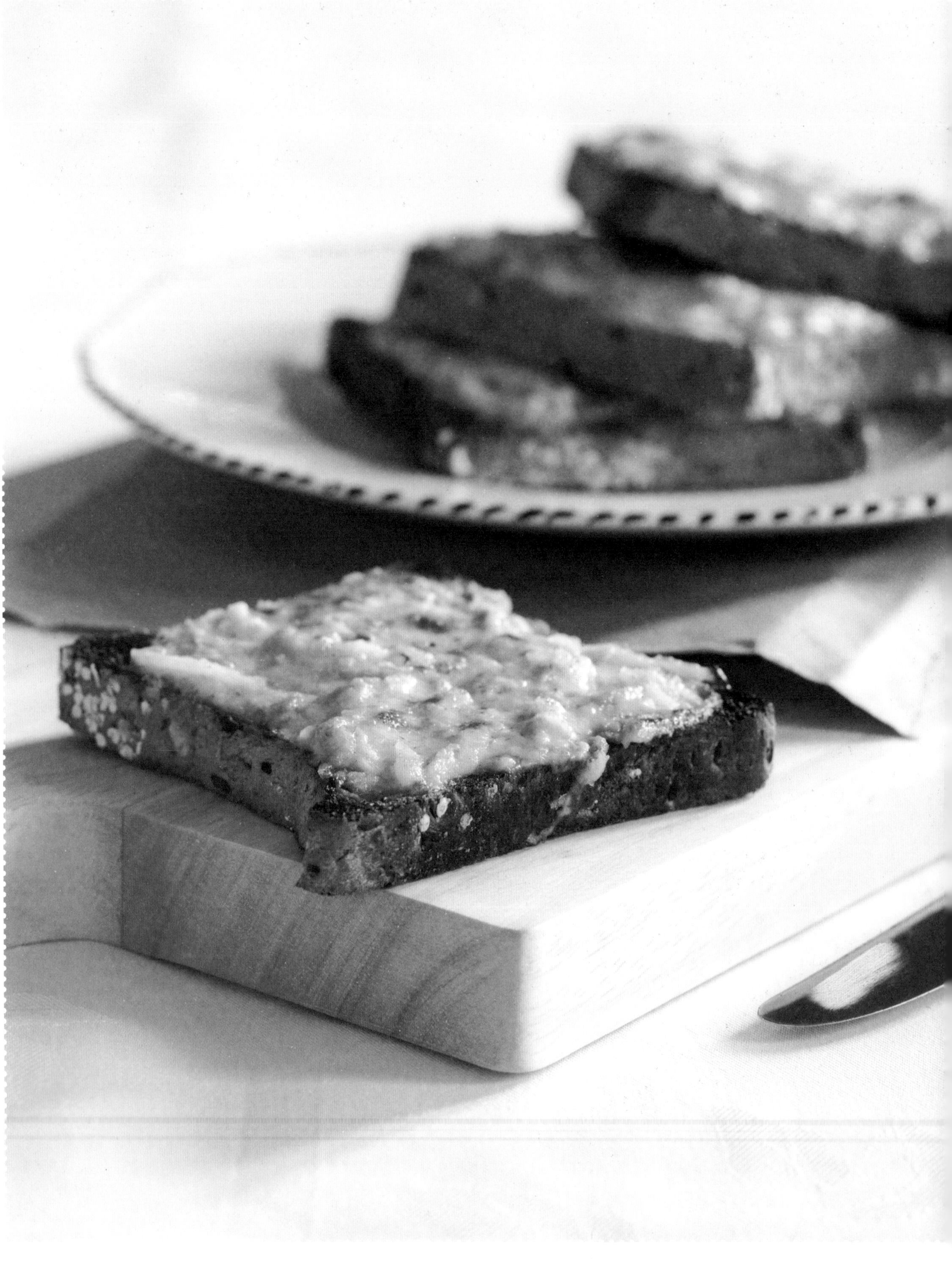

SARDINES ON TOAST

100 g sardines, drained and mashed
6 tbsp family mayo, see p. 185
¼ cup cheese, grated
1 small onion, grated
1 tsp lemon juice
1 tbsp chopped parsley
pepper
4 slices thick bread, toasted

Mix all ingredients together in a bowl, except toast. Spread the mixture evenly over the slices of toast. Grill until golden.

Serves 3–4

DAISY'S EGGS WITH HOLLANDAISE SAUCE

¼ cup milk
½ tsp salt
4 slices buttered toast, cut into rounds
4 eggs
hollandaise sauce, see p. 37

Preheat oven to 200°C.
Mix milk and salt together in a bowl. Dip toast into milk mixture and place on a greased baking tray.
Separate eggs, keeping the yolks separate from each other and whole. Beat egg whites in a large mixing bowl until stiff. Divide the egg white between the rounds of toast.
With the back of a spoon, make a place on top of the egg whites and gently position in each yolk.
Place in oven and cook for 7–10 minutes or until egg whites are golden brown.
Spoon over a little hollandaise sauce to serve.

Serves 2–4

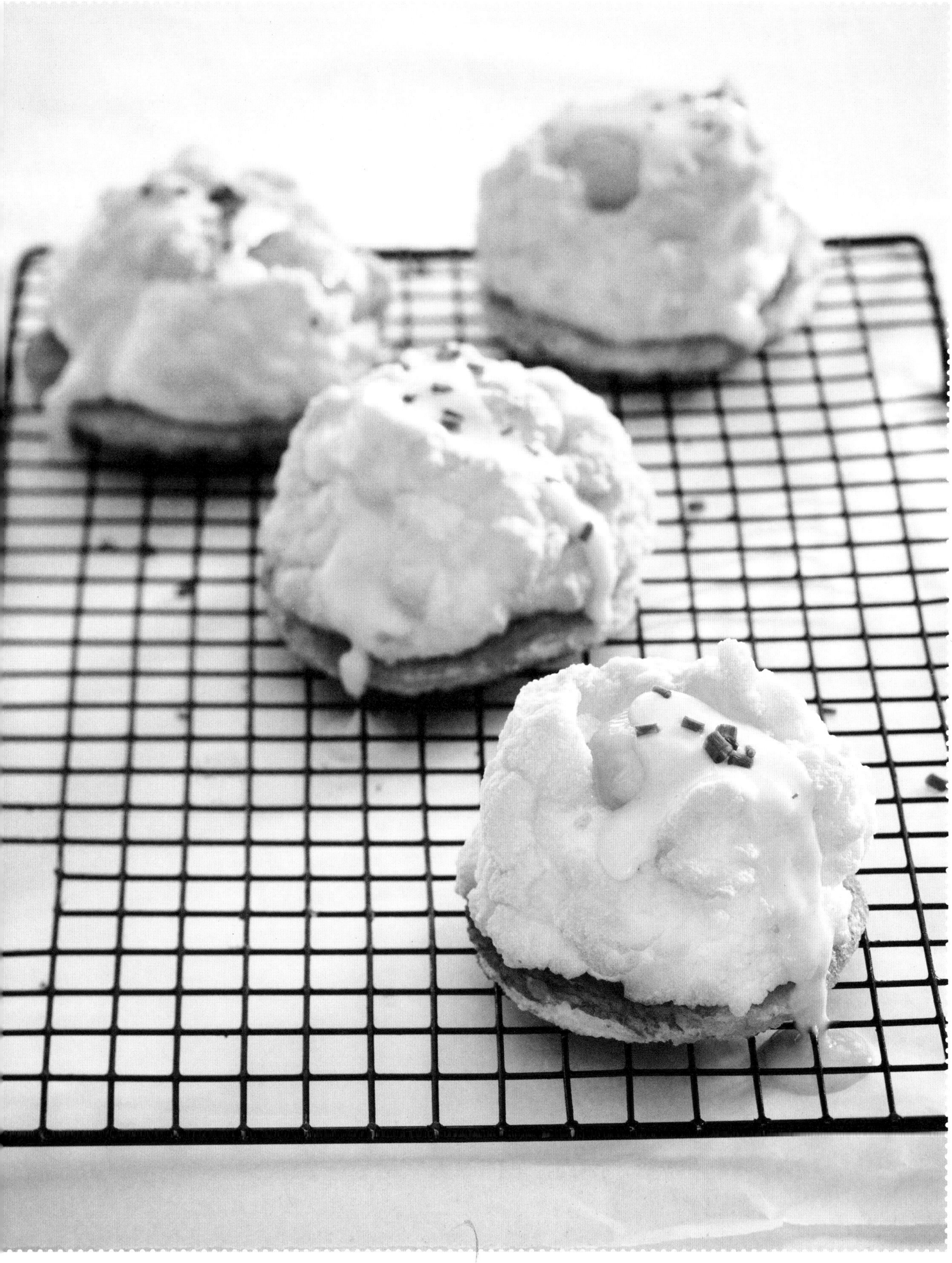

HOLLANDAISE SAUCE

25 g butter
25 g flour
200 ml milk
1 egg yolk
1 tsp lemon juice
salt and pepper

In a small saucepan melt butter, add flour and cook for 1 minute.
Slowly add milk, stirring constantly until thick.
Remove from heat and add egg yolk and lemon juice. Return to
low–medium heat and stir until thick. Season with salt and pepper.

Makes approximately 1½ cups

BREAKFAST SALAD

4 cups of your favourite salad greens
2 tomatoes, cut into small wedges
6 pieces streaky bacon, fried and cut into thirds
¼ cup fresh coriander leaves
2 tbsp sunflower oil
1 tbsp red wine vinegar
1 tbsp maple syrup
pinch of sea salt
2 poached eggs
2 slices grilled ciabatta
salt and pepper

In a medium-sized bowl, place salad greens, tomatoes, bacon and coriander.
In a separate bowl whisk together oil, vinegar and maple syrup with the pinch of sea salt. Pour into lettuce mixture and gently fold through.
Serve onto two plates and top each with a poached egg and slice of ciabatta. Season with salt and pepper.

Serves 2

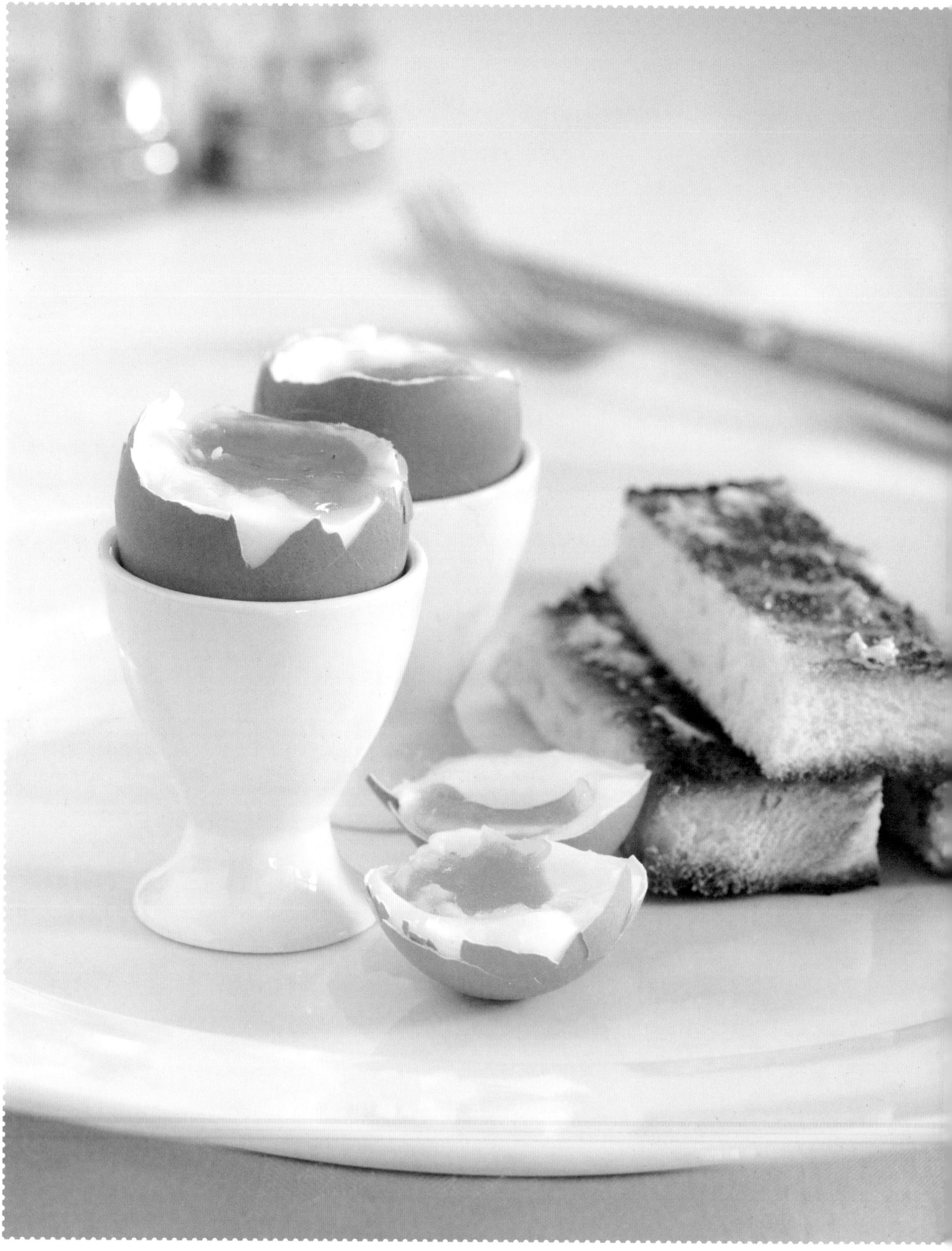

BOILED EGGS WITH SOLDIERS

4 large eggs (at room temperature)
4 slices of bread, toasted and buttered

Bring to the boil a pot three-quarters full with water. Gently lower
the eggs one at a time into the boiling water with a large spoon. Boil
according to how you like your eggs.
Runny — 5 minutes
Semi-firm — 7 minutes
Firm — 10 minutes

Once cooked, carefully remove the eggs from the water, place in egg
cups, knock off the tops with a small sharp knife and serve with hot
buttered toast cut into strips.

Serves 2

LUNCH

Lunch at Gran's was a time to relax and gather round her table to share food and fellowship. Her table was always beautifully set, and often it would just be 'the girls' dining together. As usual there would be lots to choose from. Gran's sausage rolls, hot from the oven with their sheaths of buttery flaky pastry, light, crunchy salads of garden lettuce and sweet vine tomatoes, drizzled with creamy mayonnaise, or a chunky vegetable soup with warm homemade bread. We were spoilt for choice, but willingly so!

During Gran's later years, I remember many times when my mum, my sister, my Aunty Leonie, and my daughter Gabrielle would gather in Gran's kitchen to make lunch. It was always a special treat for Gran to be able to relax and enjoy food prepared by her family — especially by her granddaughters and great-granddaughter. A poignant memory for me during that era is one of the first times I watched Gabrielle help prepare lunch at Gran's, just as I had done in that same kitchen when I was her age. I realised that my daughter was on her way to joining the family's next generation of foodlovers.

LUNCH

BACON AND ASPARAGUS SALAD

Salad

250 g bacon, chopped
1 tbsp sunflower oil
4 bunches asparagus, woody ends removed
1 tbsp chopped fresh dill
2 shallots, finely chopped
250 g mixed salad greens
¼ cup grated Parmesan

Dressing

¼ cup olive oil
1 egg yolk, lightly beaten
2 tbsp lemon juice
2 tbsp spiced vinegar, see p. 193

Fry bacon in hot oil until crisp. Drain on paper towels.
Boil a large saucepan of salted water, blanch asparagus, then run
under cold water to refresh. Dry on paper towels.
Combine dressing ingredients and mix well.
Place bacon, asparagus, dill, shallots and salad greens in a bowl, toss
through dressing, then sprinkle with Parmesan.

Serves 6

MACARONI
AND CHEESE

400 g macaroni elbows
4 tbsp butter
¼ cup flour
1½ tsp mustard powder
4 cups milk
1½ cups Cheddar
1½ cups Havarti
1 tsp Worcestershire sauce
salt and pepper
6 slices white bread
2 tbsp melted butter

Preheat oven to 200°C.
Bring a large saucepan of salted water to the boil. Add macaroni and
cook for 10 minutes or until *al dente*, then drain pasta.
While macaroni is cooking, melt the 4 tablespoons of butter in a
large saucepan over a low heat. Once melted, add flour and mustard
powder and cook for 1–2 minutes, stirring constantly. Whisk in milk,
1 cup at a time, and bring to the boil. Reduce heat and simmer until
sauce thickens. This should take about 3–4 minutes.
Remove sauce from heat and add cheeses, Worcestershire sauce and
macaroni. Season with salt and pepper. Place in a large baking dish
and set aside.
Place bread in food processor and pulse to make coarse breadcrumbs.
Add melted butter and pulse.
Sprinkle crumbs over top of macaroni and bake for 20 minutes.

Serves 4–6

SAVOURY TOAST

1 cup grated cheese
1 tsp Worcestershire sauce
1 tbsp tomato sauce
⅛ tsp cayenne pepper
4 thick slices buttered bread

Preheat oven to 190°C.
Place all ingredients in a bowl (except bread) and stir gently to
combine. Spread the mixture evenly over the bread. Place on lined
baking tray and cook for 15–20 minutes until bubbly and golden.

Serves 2–3

TOMATO AND EGG PIE

shortcrust pastry, see p. 68
50 g butter
1 small onion, diced
50 g flour
400 ml milk
salt and pepper
6 vine tomatoes, halved
4 hard-boiled eggs, quartered
½ cup grated cheese

Preheat oven to 200°C.
Roll out pastry and press it into a 23-cm pie dish. Blind-bake pastry for 15 minutes. Remove from oven and set aside to cool.
Melt butter in a medium-sized saucepan, add diced onion and gently sauté for 1–2 minutes. Add flour and cook for a further 1–2 minutes. Slowly add milk, stirring continuously until thick, and season with salt and pepper.
Add tomatoes and eggs. Pour into cooled pastry case, sprinkle with grated cheese and bake for 20 minutes.

Serves 6–8

GREEN SOUP

3 tbsp olive oil
3 medium-sized onions, diced
1 leek, sliced
6 large courgettes, roughly chopped
400 g watercress, roughly chopped
3 litres chicken stock
salt and pepper
small pinch of saffron

Place a large saucepan over a medium heat and add olive oil. Add
onions and leek and sauté for 5–6 minutes until soft. Add courgettes,
watercress and chicken stock and cook for a further 10 minutes.
Season with salt and pepper.
Cool to room temperature then place in a blender or food processor
and purée. Reheat to serve. Garnish with saffron.

Serves 6–8

CHICKEN AND GINGER ROLLS

500 g minced chicken
1 tsp salt
2 tbsp finely chopped coriander
2 tbsp finely grated ginger
zest of 1 lemon
2 eggs, lightly beaten
1 cup breadcrumbs
2 sheets ready-rolled flaky pastry
¼ cup flour
a little milk for brushing

Preheat oven to 200°C.
Place chicken, salt, coriander, ginger, lemon zest, eggs and breadcrumbs in a bowl and mix well until combined.
Divide mixture in half, shape meat mixture into rolls the length of the pastry sheets and roll them in flour. Place each pastry sheet separately on flat surface and wet one edge of the pastry so that the meat will stick to it. Then place meat on the damp area and roll up the pastry sheet to form a log. Cut into desired sizes and brush each sausage roll with milk.
Cook for approximately 20 minutes, or until golden brown and cooked thoroughly.

Makes around 10

DEVILLED TOMATO

3 large tomatoes
1 tbsp softened butter
1 tsp mustard powder
1 tbsp grated cheese
pinch of black pepper
1 tbsp vinegar

Preheat oven to 200°C.
Cut tomatoes in half and place on baking tray. Mix butter, mustard powder, grated cheese, pepper and vinegar. Spread paste over cut surface of tomatoes and bake for 30 minutes.
Serve with fresh bread and cold meats.

Serves 3–4

PUMPKIN TART

shortcrust pastry, see p. 68
½ medium-sized pumpkin, peeled, chopped and cooked
4 eggs
500 ml cream
salt and pepper
1 cup sour cream
2 tbsp finely chopped chives

Preheat oven to 200°C.
Roll out and line a 23-cm flan tin with pastry.
Mash pumpkin in a large bowl, add eggs, cream, salt and pepper and
stir vigorously for 1–2 minutes. Pour into pastry base and cook for
30–40 minutes or until set.
Mix sour cream and chives together and serve with warm tart.

Serves 6–8

SMOKED TREVALLY PÂTÉ

400 g smoked trevally
100 g very soft butter
zest and juice of 1 lemon
2 tbsp parsley
125 g sour cream
salt and pepper

Flake smoked fish into a mixing bowl. Add butter, lemon zest and juice and parsley. Beat until creamy. Fold through sour cream and season with salt and pepper.

Serves 3–4

SAUSAGES

500 g minced beef
250 g minced pork
1 onion, grated
¼ cup finely chopped fresh thyme
1 tbsp salt
2 tbsp sunflower oil

Mix all ingredients except oil together until well combined. Divide mixture into 10 portions and form into approximately 9-cm-long sausages.
Heat oil in a frying-pan and fry sausages on all sides until golden and cooked through.

Makes 10

SWEETCORN CHOWDER

50 g butter
4 small-sized onions, diced
4 medium-sized potatoes, diced
4 tomatoes, diced
800 g creamed corn
1 litre chicken stock

Melt butter in a large saucepan. Add onions and fry for about
5 minutes. Add potatoes and tomatoes and cook for 3–4 minutes.
Add corn and stock. Simmer for 20–25 minutes.

Serves 6–8

SHORTCRUST PASTRY

50 g butter
100 g flour
1 egg yolk, lightly beaten
10–15 ml cold water

Place butter and flour in food processor and pulse until crumbly.
Add egg yolk while food processor is still running. Add a little cold
water to form a dough ball. Cover with plastic food wrap and chill
for 30 minutes before using.

DINNER

Dinnertime in our family was and still is an opportunity to relax after a busy day, gather together, share delicious food and take the time to listen to one another. The evening mealtime is also a great opportunity for celebration, whether it is someone's birthday, an anniversary or a festive Christmas dinner.

When I was a child, all meals at Gran's felt like a celebration. The table was always laden with fresh produce from Gran and Pop's garden and orchard, which had been transformed into mouthwatering dishes in Gran's cosy kitchen. Golden roast chicken with stuffing; succulent meatloaf served with fluffy mashed potatoes, steamed green beans and velvety rich gravy; or a tender beef casserole, ladled over sweet golden kumara and pumpkin mash. The air would be filled with the wafting aromas of Gran's creations. My grandmother certainly knew how to create a special atmosphere in the midst of the ordinary.

As young girls we would often help Gran prepare the food, but the true highlight for me was standing beside my Pop when he carved the meat or chicken. I would stealthily remove morsels from the carving dish, into my mouth. Pop would allow me to do this, unbeknown to my siblings, and that made me feel very special. Pop was a very reserved man at heart, but he loved food and he knew how to indulge a fellow foodlover. I can still see his cheeky smile, with those big blue eyes looking down at me.

DINNER

BEEF CASSEROLE WITH WALNUT DUMPLINGS

Beef casserole
2 tbsp olive oil
1 kg gravy beef
1 onion, diced
2 cloves garlic, crushed
250 g mushrooms, sliced
250 g bacon, diced
2 tbsp plain flour
2½ cups beef stock
½ cup red wine
2 tbsp thyme, chopped
salt and pepper

Walnut dumplings
200 g self-raising flour
50 g butter, diced
100 g walnuts, chopped
salt and pepper
5 tbsp milk

To make casserole, heat oil in a large saucepan, then add beef and brown. Set meat aside.

Using the same saucepan, fry onion, garlic, mushrooms and bacon for 5 minutes. Stir in flour. Return beef to saucepan and stir.

Slowly pour in stock and wine, then add thyme. Bring to the boil, cover, reduce heat and simmer for 1½ hours. Season with salt and pepper.

To make dumplings, place flour and butter in a food processor and pulse until crumbly. Tip into a bowl. Add walnuts, salt and pepper and gently stir in the milk to make a soft dough.

Roll out the dough onto a floured surface to 2 cm thick and cut out 8 rounds using a 6-cm cutter.

When casserole is cooked, stir, then place dumplings on top, starting around edge of saucepan, working your way into the middle until fully covered. Cover saucepan with a lid and simmer for 20–25 minutes until dumplings risen and cooked.

Serves 6–8

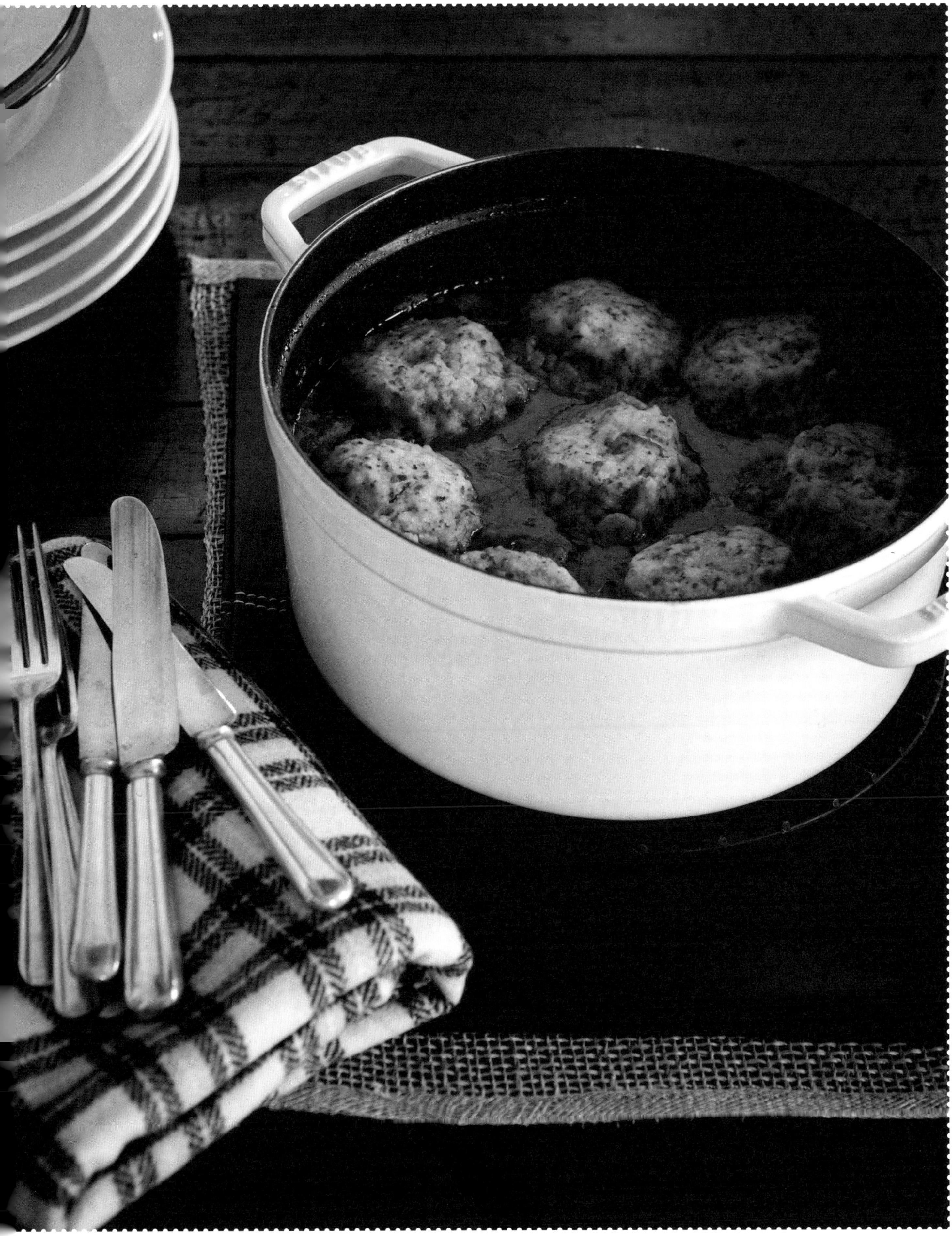

BACON, SPINACH AND BARLEY SOUP

2 tbsp oil
1 medium-sized onion, diced
1 medium-sized carrot, diced
3 sticks celery, diced
2 bacon hocks
1 cup washed barley
4 bay leaves
3 cups baby spinach
zest and juice of 1 lemon
salt and pepper

Heat oil in a large saucepan and sauté onion, carrot and celery for 8–10 minutes until soft. Add hocks, barley and bay leaves. Cover with a generous amount of water, bring to the boil and simmer for 2 hours with the lid on.
Remove bay leaves, bones and any large pieces of meat. Chop meat and return to saucepan, adding spinach, lemon zest and juice, and salt and pepper to taste.

Serves 4–6

MARINATED LAMB

10 lamb shoulder chops

Marinade
⅓ cup Worcestershire sauce
⅓ cup soy sauce
⅓ cup brown sugar
⅓ cup dark rum
1 onion, grated
2 tbsp mustard powder
2 tbsp tomato paste
2 cloves garlic, crushed
2 tbsp sunflower oil
2 tbsp fresh ginger, grated
1 tsp ground coriander
1 tsp ground allspice
1 tsp ground nutmeg
zest and juice of 1 lemon
zest and juice of 1 orange
salt and pepper

Mix marinade ingredients in a saucepan and bring to the boil, stirring until sugar dissolves. Simmer for 4–5 minutes. Cool.
Place lamb in dish, pour over marinade and coat well. Cover and leave in the fridge for 24 hours.
Grill or barbecue to your liking. Rest for 5 minutes before serving.

Serves 6–8

ROAST LEEK AND LEMON CHICKEN THIGHS

6 large leeks, roughly sliced
4 large carrots, peeled and roughly sliced
8 chicken thighs
10 cloves garlic, unpeeled
6 bay leaves
4 sprigs thyme
1 tbsp olive oil
zest and juice of 1 lemon
150 ml white wine
salt and pepper

Preheat oven to 180°C.
Place leeks and carrots in the bottom of a roasting tray. Arrange chicken, garlic, bay leaves and thyme on top. Drizzle over olive oil, lemon zest and juice and wine. Season with salt and pepper. Cover with tin foil and bake for 45 minutes.
Remove from oven and increase heat to 220°C. Remove foil and return to oven to brown for 15–20 minutes.

Serves 6–8

CORNED BEEF WITH MUSTARD SAUCE

Corned beef

1.5 kg piece corned silverside
1 tbsp brown sugar
1 tbsp malt vinegar
1 onion, roughly chopped
1 tsp black peppercorns

Mustard sauce

¾ cup sugar
½ cup vinegar
½ cup stock
½ tsp pepper
1 tsp mustard
1 egg

3 bay leaves to garnish

To cook the corned beef, place the silverside in a large saucepan and cover with water. Add remaining ingredients and bring to the boil. Reduce to a simmer and cover and cook for 1½ hours.
To make the mustard sauce, combine all ingredients in a medium-sized saucepan. Slowly bring to the boil, stirring continuously.

Serves 6–8

SAUSAGE PIE

1 large onion, diced
1 tbsp butter
1 kg sausage meat
3 tomatoes, sliced
410 g can spaghetti
500 g mashed potatoes
½ cup grated cheese

Preheat oven to 190°C.
Sauté onion in butter until soft.
Press 500 g of sausage meat into a deep dish. Layer with onion, tomatoes and spaghetti. Roll out remaining sausage meat on floured surface to the size of the dish. Place on top of spaghetti. Top with mashed potatoes then sprinkle with grated cheese. Bake for 45–50 minutes or until golden brown.

Serves 6–8

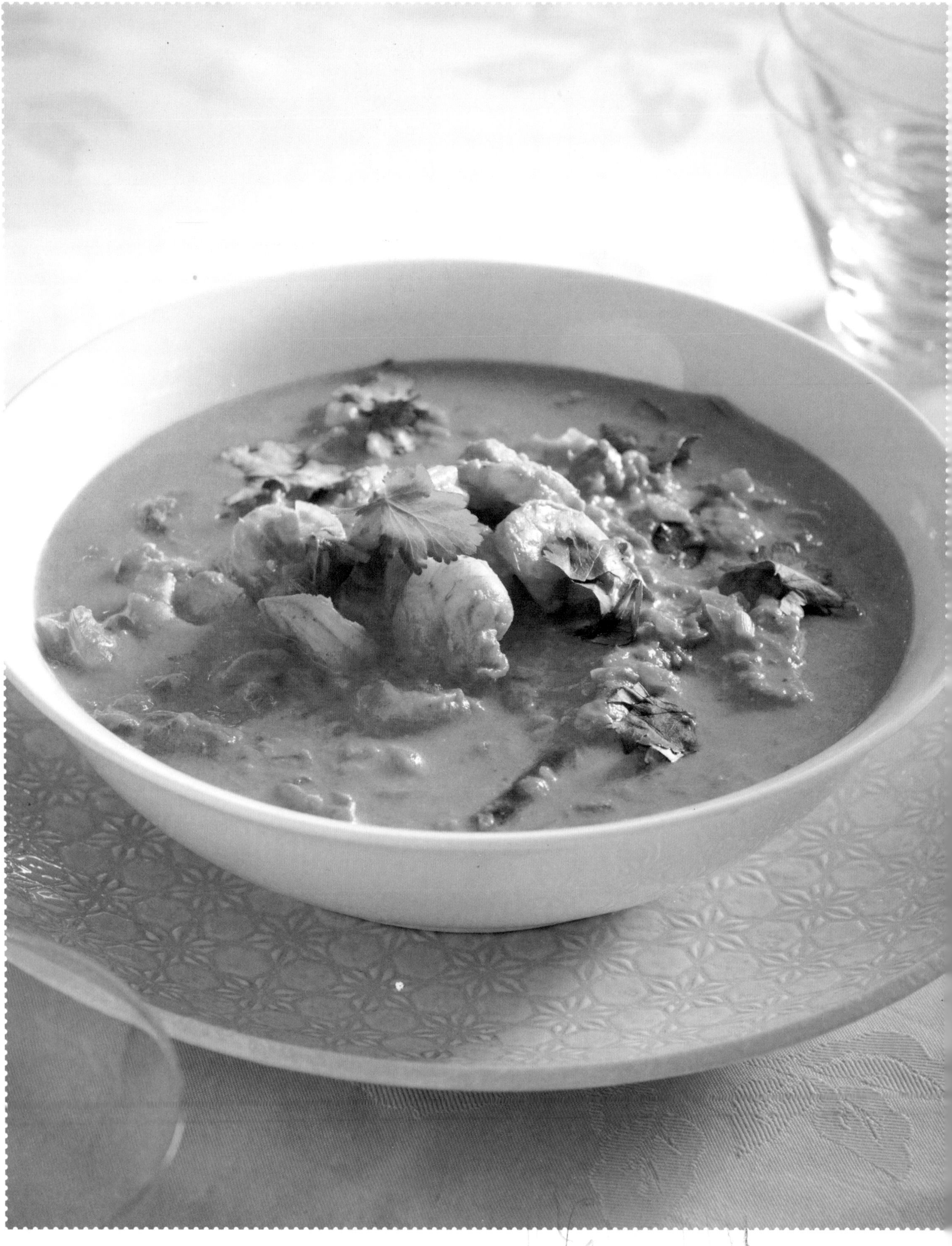

PRAWN CURRY

1 tbsp peanut oil
1 onion, diced
1 tsp ground coriander
3 tsp turmeric
1 tsp nutmeg
¼ tsp chilli powder
1 cinnamon stick
1 large clove garlic, crushed
5-cm piece of fresh ginger, peeled and finely chopped
4 green chillies, seeded and finely chopped
30 curry leaves
410 ml coconut milk
410 g chopped tomatoes
zest and juice of 1 lemon
100 ml water
1 tbsp sugar
2 tsp salt
500 g raw prawns, deveined and shelled
1 bunch fresh coriander, roughly chopped

Heat oil in a large saucepan and fry onion until soft. Add coriander,
turmeric, nutmeg, chilli powder, cinnamon stick, garlic, ginger,
chillies and curry leaves. Cook for 5–6 minutes.
Add coconut milk, tomatoes, lemon zest and juice, water, sugar
and salt and bring to the boil. Reduce heat and simmer for 15–20
minutes.
Add prawns and return to the boil. Cook for 5–8 minutes until
prawns are cooked.
Garnish with fresh coriander.

Serves 4–6

BEEF OLIVES

1 cup breadcrumbs
1 cup prunes
1 large onion, finely chopped
1 tsp lemon zest
1 tsp thyme
6 pieces beef schnitzel
4 tbsp oil
4 tbsp plain flour
3 cups beef stock
4 tbsp Worcestershire sauce

Preheat oven to 160°C.
Combine breadcrumbs, prunes, onion, lemon zest and thyme.
Lay pieces of schnitzel out flat. Spread each piece of meat with
breadcrumb mixture then roll up like a sponge roll. Secure with
toothpicks.
Heat oil in frying-pan. Add beef olives and brown on all sides.
Transfer to casserole dish.
Add flour to the same frying-pan and cook for 1 minute. Gradually
add stock, stirring constantly. Bring to boil. Add Worcestershire
sauce. Pour over beef olives. Cook at 160°C for 45 minutes or until
meat is tender. Remove toothpicks before serving.

Serves 4–6

GRILLED SNAPPER WITH BAKED ONIONS

16 pickling onions
salt and pepper
600 ml cream
250 g Gruyère, grated
¼ cup flour
¼ cup milk
4 snapper fillets
6 tbsp olive oil
lemon wedges

Preheat oven to 160°C.

Peel onions and boil in a saucepan of water for 20–25 minutes, or until soft.

Drain onions, then place in a casserole dish and season with salt and pepper. Add cream to dish and sprinkle with cheese. Bake for 25–30 minutes.

Season flour with salt and pepper and sprinkle over a work surface. Place milk in a wide, shallow bowl. Dip snapper fillets into milk, then transfer to seasoned flour and coat each fillet.

When baked onions are almost ready, pan-fry snapper fillets in olive oil for 5 minutes on each side (depending on thickness of fillets).

Serve snapper fillets on a bed of baked onions with a lemon wedge on the side.

Serves 4–6

GOLDEN SAUSAGES

6 pork sausages
1 carrot, grated
1 onion, diced
4 tbsp tomato sauce
3 tbsp flour
3 tbsp white vinegar
3 tbsp brown sugar
4 tbsp Worcestershire sauce
2 tbsp chopped parsley
2 cups boiling water
salt and pepper

Preheat oven to 170°C.
Place sausages, carrot and onion in a casserole dish. Mix together all
other ingredients and pour over sausages. Cover and cook for 2 hours.

Serves 4–6

HAM ON THE BONE WITH TANGELO AND MUSTARD GLAZE

7–8 kg ham hock, skin removed
60 g black peppercorns or cloves

Tangelo and mustard glaze
1 cup tangelo marmalade or traditional marmalade
2 tbsp Dijon mustard
¼ cup brandy
¾ cup brown sugar

Preheat oven to 200°C.

Score flesh of ham in a diamond pattern with a knife. Place a clove or peppercorn in the corner of each diamond. Cover ham with tin foil to prevent it from burning.

To make the glaze, place all ingredients in a saucepan and stir over a low heat until sugar is dissolved. Bring to the boil and simmer for 8–10 minutes, or until the mixture becomes thick.

Place ham in a roasting dish lined with baking paper and brush with glaze. Roast ham for 1½ hours, basting with glaze every 15 minutes.

MEAT LOAF

410 g can tomato purée
400 g minced beef
100 g minced pork
30 g rolled oats
1 onion, diced
1 clove garlic, crushed
1 tbsp parsley, chopped
50 ml red wine
1 tsp sugar
½ tsp pepper

Preheat oven to 180°C.
In a large bowl, mix together half the tomato purée with remaining ingredients and mix well.
Grease a 25 x 10 cm loaf tin. Press meat mixture into the tin and pour on the rest of the tomato purée. Bake for 1 hour.

Serves 4–6

SLOW ROAST PORK SHOULDER

2.5–3 kg pork shoulder, bone in
salt and pepper
apple sauce, see p. 176

Preheat oven to 220°C.
Place pork shoulder in a large roasting dish. Score skin. Season with salt and pepper, rubbing into incisions.
Roast for 40–45 minutes, or until skin is golden and crackling, then reduce heat to 170°C. Cover pork snugly with a double layer of tin foil, return to oven and cook for 4 hours, basting occasionally with pan juices.
Uncover and return to oven to cook for another hour.
Serve with apple sauce.

Serves 8–10

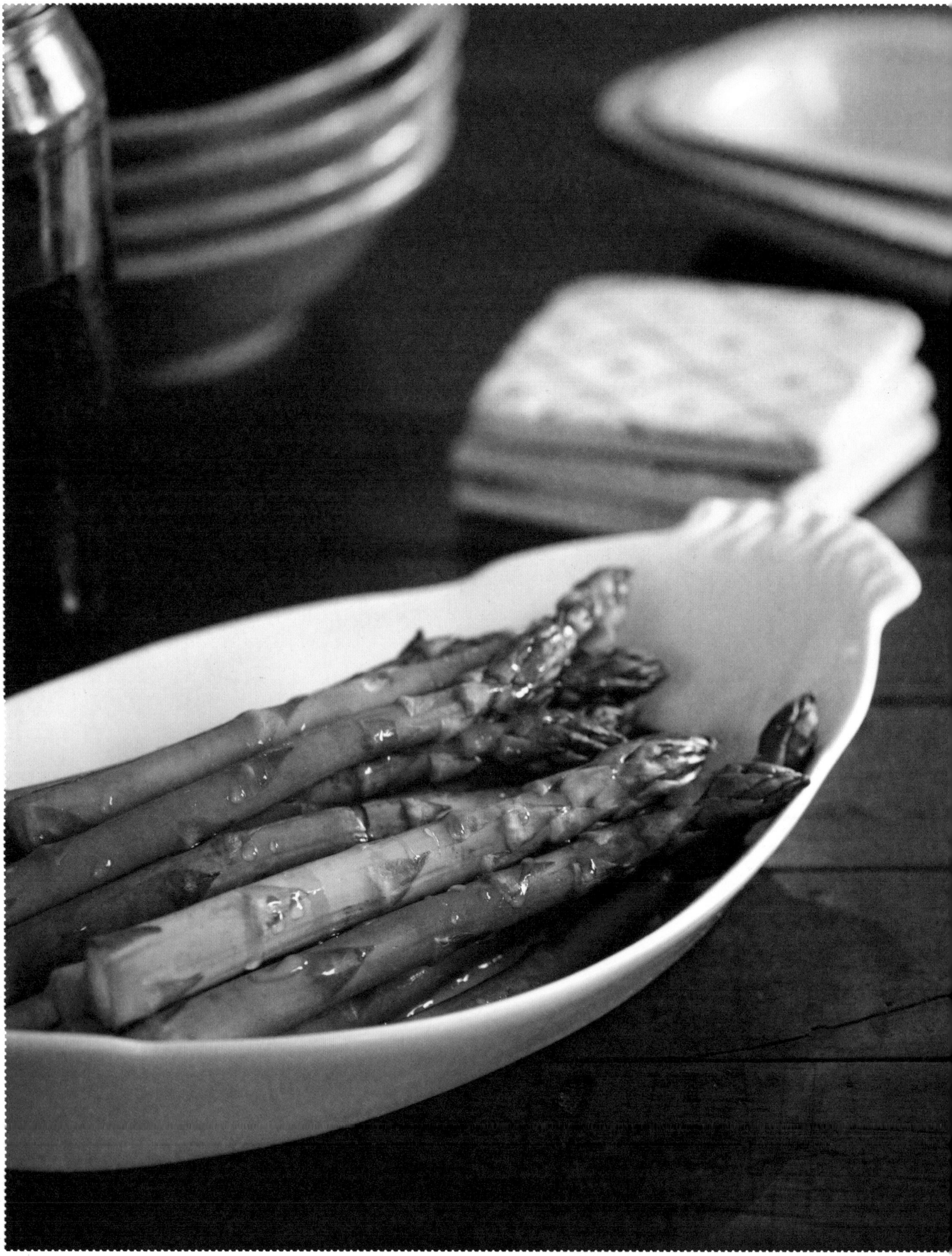

SALADS AND SIDES

I remember, as though it were yesterday, the ripe earthy smells of my grandparents' vegetable garden; losing myself in the hothouse full of juicy red vine tomatoes; the pungent smokiness of manuka and fish wafting from the smokehouse; the heady sweetness of blossoms on the fruit trees; and the sweet syrupy scent of plump ripe strawberries. These are the fragrances and aromas of my childhood.

As children, my sister, brother and I were often sent outside to play in the rambling backyard and garden at Gran and Pop's Weymouth home. We used to have so much fun, running around the large section, past the smokehouse where the morning's catch would be sizzling away, and around the huge vegetable garden, where we would pick sweet crunchy beans straight off the vine, to snack on before dinner. We would always check with Pop to see how many beans we were each allowed while we were out on our adventures. We would be so ravenous, as we often stayed outside for hours playing games, including my favourite, 'Go home, stay home'. Then Gran would ring the bell that signalled dinner was ready.

I loved the way Gran always had salads and sides to accompany her meals. Summer was always my favourite time of year as she would make delicious salads. Juicy ripe hothouse tomatoes would sit alongside crunchy lettuces and cucumbers, crisp carrots and tangy beetroot. Gran's motto was always that variety was the key, so it was good to be able to have a little bit of everything. Maybe she liked to have lots of dishes to choose from so everyone would find something they liked, or perhaps she couldn't decide what her favourite dishes were as she had so many. Whatever the reason, our meals were always full of amazing flavours, colours and textures, and we felt thoroughly satisfied after every meal.

SALADS AND SIDES

CAULIFLOWER CHEESE

1 tbsp salt
2 small cauliflowers
50 g butter
50 g plain flour
800 ml milk
2 tsp wholegrain mustard
1½ tsp ground nutmeg
75 g grated Cheddar cheese, plus a bit extra for sprinkling over top
salt and pepper

Preheat oven to 180°C.
Place a large saucepan of salted water over a high temperature and bring to the boil. Place whole cauliflowers in the saucepan and boil for 15 minutes. Cool cauliflowers under cold running water, drain and set aside.
Melt butter in a medium-sized saucepan and add flour. Cook over a medium heat for 3–4 minutes, stirring continuously. Slowly add milk, still stirring continuously, and bring to the boil.
Add mustard, nutmeg and cheese. Season to taste.
Place whole cauliflowers in an ovenproof dish. Pour over white sauce, sprinkle with extra grated cheese and bake for 30–40 minutes until soft and golden.

Serves 6

BOWL OF COOKED GREENS

2 heads broccoli
1 cup frozen peas
salt and pepper

Cut broccoli into florets and boil in hot water until tender. Add frozen peas and boil for a further 30 seconds. Drain and season with salt and pepper.

Serves 4–6

CRUNCHY ROAST POTATOES

1.5 kg medium-sized Agria potatoes
4 tbsp olive oil
1 tsp salt

Preheat oven to 200°C.
Bring a large saucepan of water to the boil. Add potatoes and boil for
10 minutes. Run under cold water and set aside until cool. Peel, then
cut in half.
Place oil in roasting pan and heat for 10 minutes. While oil is
heating, scrape potatoes with a fork to create a rough surface.
Place potatoes carefully in roasting pan and gently toss until they are
coated on all sides. Sprinkle with salt, return to oven and bake for
1 hour or until golden on all sides. Turn 3–4 times during roasting.

Serves 6–8

COLESLAW

½ medium-sized cabbage, finely shredded
1 carrot, grated
¼ cup finely chopped mint
1 red apple, diced
¼ cup family mayo, see p. 185

Combine all ingredients in a salad bowl. Toss well to combine,
and serve.

Serves 4–6

CUCUMBER AND TOMATO SALAD

1 small red onion, finely sliced
4 large tomatoes, peeled and sliced
1 cucumber, peeled and sliced
1 tbsp sugar
½ cup boiling water
⅓ cup malt vinegar
salt and pepper

Place onion, tomatoes and cucumber in a bowl. For the dressing, put sugar into a small bowl, pour in boiling water and stir until sugar has dissolved. Add vinegar, season with salt and pepper then pour over vegetables.

Serves 2–4

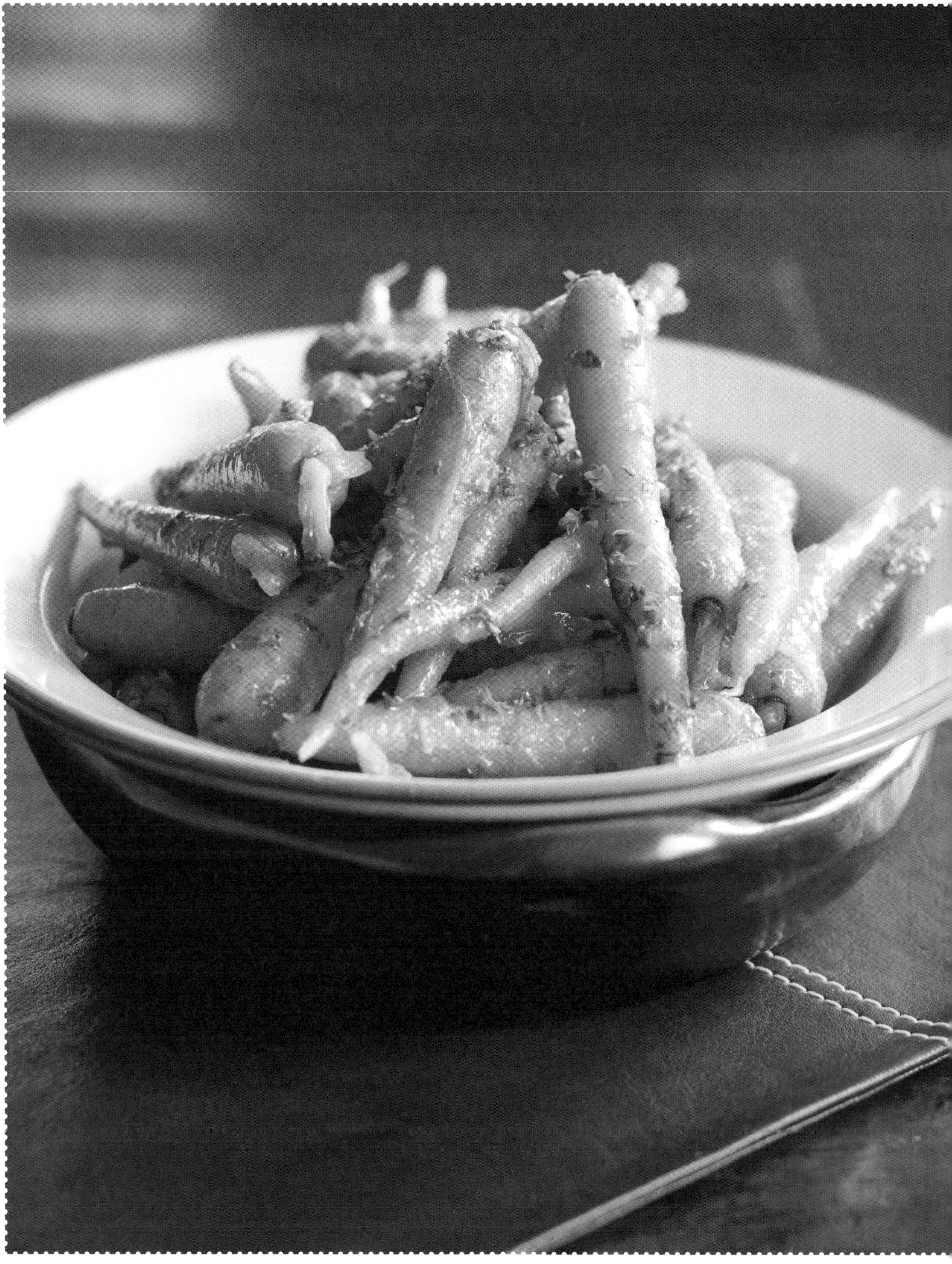

GLAZED BABY CARROTS

20 baby carrots
1 tsp salt
40 g butter
1 tbsp honey
2 tbsp finely chopped fresh parsley

Cook carrots in a saucepan of salted boiling water for 5 minutes, then refresh immediately in cold water.
Melt butter and honey in a frying-pan. Add carrots and toss until hot.
Add parsley and serve.

Serves 4–6

COOKED BEETROOT

6 medium-sized beetroot

Dressing
4 tbsp white sugar
pinch of salt
1½ cups boiling water
½ cup malt vinegar

Add whole, unpeeled beetroot to a saucepan of boiling water. Boil for approximately 30–40 minutes, or until soft in the middle. When cool enough to hold, peel, slice into rounds and place in a bowl.
To make the dressing, combine sugar and salt in a bowl. Pour over boiling water and stir until dissolved. Add vinegar, mix together and pour over beetroot.

Serves 4–6

GREEN SALAD

1 iceberg lettuce
1 large radish, thinly sliced
40 ml red wine vinegar
75 ml olive oil
1 tsp Dijon mustard
1 tbsp sugar
1 tsp salt
1 tbsp chopped parsley
salt and pepper

Wash and dry lettuce leaves and place in a bowl. Slice radish thinly and place on lettuce.
Whisk vinegar, oil, mustard, sugar and salt together. Stir in parsley.
Pour dressing over salad and season with salt and pepper.

Serves 4–6

KUMARA WITH GINGER, ORANGE AND CHIVES

4 medium-sized red kumara
30 g peeled fresh ginger
120 g soft butter
zest of 1 orange
30 g chives, chopped
salt and pepper

Preheat oven to 190°C.
Wash and dry kumara. Prick the skins and place on greased baking tray. Bake for 40–60 minutes or until kumara is soft in the middle and skin is crispy.
While kumara is cooling, finely grate ginger, then cream it with butter, orange zest, chives, salt and pepper.
Halve the kumara lengthways, then arrange on platter or plate. Top each half with a generous helping of butter mix.

Serves 6–8

MASHED POTATOES

1 kg Agria potatoes, peeled and cut into quarters
1 tbsp salt
50 g butter
1 tbsp olive oil
175 ml milk
salt and pepper
½ tsp grated nutmeg

Place potatoes in boiling salted water. Continue boiling until cooked, then drain and mash.
Add butter and oil, then milk. Season with salt, pepper and nutmeg.

Serves 4–6

MASHED ROOT VEGETABLES

1.5 kg root vegetables (e.g. carrots, potatoes, kumara, parsnips),
    peeled and roughly chopped
3 cloves garlic
1 tbsp salt
1 cup cream
¼ cup butter
handful of fresh thyme
handful of fresh rosemary
2 bay leaves
salt and pepper
bunch of fresh chives, chopped

Place root vegetables and garlic in a saucepan full of cold water, until
vegetables are just covered. Add salt.

Bring to the boil and simmer for about 30 minutes, or until tender.
While vegetables are cooking, combine cream, butter, thyme,
rosemary and bay leaves in a saucepan. Heat to melt butter but do
not allow to boil. Turn off heat, cover and let herbs infuse until ready
to use, then drain.

Drain vegetables and mash. Stir in warm cream mixture and mix
until combined and vegetables are smooth. Season with salt and
pepper. Garnish with fresh chives.

Serves 6–8

PARSLEY COUSCOUS

250 ml water
250 g couscous
40 g butter
salt and pepper
30 g fresh parsley, chopped

Place water in a saucepan with a little salt and bring to the boil.
Remove from heat and stir in couscous. Cover and set aside for
2–3 minutes.
Return to low heat. Stir in butter with a fork. Season with salt and
pepper, then add the parsley. Serve immediately.

Serves 4–6

POTATO SALAD IN RED WINE VINEGAR

8 medium-sized potatoes, peeled and cubed
¼ cup red wine vinegar
2 tbsp chopped dill
⅓ cup sour cream
⅓ cup family mayo, see p. 185
salt and pepper
2 small red onions, thinly sliced

Place potatoes in a large saucepan of salted water set on a low heat, bring to the boil and cook until tender. Drain.
Gently toss potatoes with vinegar and dill and set aside to cool.
Combine sour cream and mayonnaise. Season with salt and pepper.
Add red onions and gently fold into potatoes.

Serves 6

POTATO SCONES

2 Agria potatoes, cooked and mashed through a ricer
400 g plain flour
50 g butter, grated
½ tsp salt
2 tbsp baking powder
250 ml milk

Preheat oven to 220°C.
Place mashed potatoes, flour, grated butter, salt and baking powder in a bowl and stir in milk.
Knead together gently to form a dough. Roll out on floured surface and cut out rounds with a 7–9-cm scone cutter. Place on greased baking tray and bake for 15–20 minutes or until golden brown.

Makes 15–20

ROASTED ASPARAGUS

1 kg asparagus, woody ends removed
4 cloves garlic, peeled and sliced
50 ml olive oil
salt and pepper
15 fresh basil leaves, torn

Preheat oven to 230°C.
Wash asparagus under cold water and stand in colander to drip off
excess water. Place in roasting dish. Add garlic, olive oil, salt and
pepper and shake dish to ensure asparagus is well coated in oil.
Roast for 10–15 minutes, depending on thickness of asparagus. Add
basil and serve.

Serves 6–8

RUSTIC CHIPS

50 ml olive oil
6 large potatoes, washed, dried and cut into wedges
30 g wholemeal flour
salt and pepper

Preheat oven to 230°C.
Pour oil into large roasting dish and heat for about 5 minutes.
Cut potatoes into wedges and toss in flour, salt and pepper. Place potatoes in roasting pan in a single layer.
Bake for 40–45 minutes until golden and crunchy. Shake roasting pan throughout cooking process to avoid sticking.

Serves 6

SPECIAL BEAN SALAD

2 x 425 g tins of four bean mix, drained
1 cup chopped celery
1 small red onion, finely diced
¼ cup sweet chutney
¼ cup sunflower oil
2 tbsp white vinegar
½ tsp mustard powder
salt and pepper

Combine beans, celery, onion and chutney in a bowl.
Whisk together oil, vinegar, mustard powder, salt and pepper.
Pour dressing over vegetables and toss gently.

Serves 6

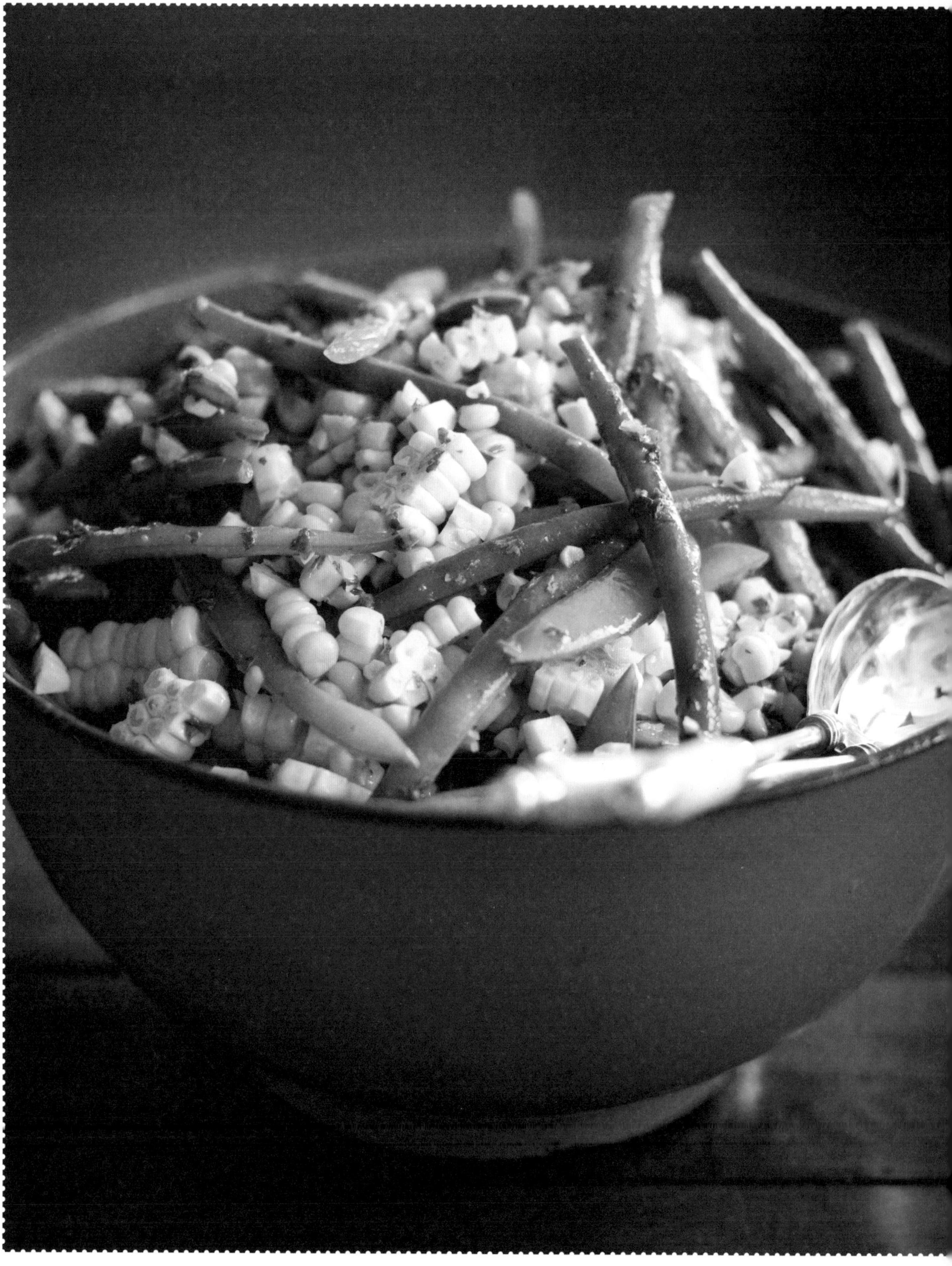

SUMMER SALAD WITH LEMON HERB DRESSING

Summer salad
350 g flat green beans
350 g round green beans
150 g sugar snap peas
2 corn cobs

Lemon herb dressing
⅓ cup mint leaves
½ cup parsley
zest and juice of 1 lemon
¼ cup olive oil
salt and pepper

To make the salad, bring a saucepan of salted water to the boil. Blanch each vegetable separately, then drop into iced water and dry on paper towels. Slice corn kernels from blanched cobs in large chunks.
To make the dressing, place all ingredients in a food processor and pulse until well combined. Season to taste.
Mix beans, sugar snaps and dressing in a bowl, then gently mix in corn.

Serves 4–6

PUDDINGS

Since childhood my favourite time of day has always been pudding time. Nothing tantalises my taste buds more than the arrival of a delicious pudding on the table. It's the dramatic finale to the dining experience, and has been a long-standing tradition in our family life, whether it was at Gran and Pop's, or at home with my own parents. Pudding was never overlooked.

I remember the serving of pudding as being the quietest part of the meal when I was young. We would eagerly lower our spoons into soft, spongy steamed puddings dripping with custard, and into old-fashioned lemon delicious, smothered in whipped cream. Whatever form it took, pudding was always the perfect end to any day. These are memories I cherish.

These days, with my own family, pudding remains just as important and revered — whether it be a luxurious hot, self-saucing pudding in winter, or a simple fresh fruit salad and homemade ice cream on a hot summer night. The proof, so they say, is always in the pudding.

PUDDINGS

APPLE CRISP

4 large cooking apples, peeled and sliced
¾ cup cold water
¼ tsp cinnamon
½ cup sugar
¾ cup flour
50 g butter

Preheat oven to 190°C.
Place apples in casserole dish, pour over cold water and sprinkle
with cinnamon.
Rub together sugar, flour and butter until crumbly. Place on top
of apple.
Bake for 40 minutes. Serve hot or cold.

Serves 4–6

LEMON BAVARIAN CREAM

2 packets lemon jelly crystals
2 cups boiling water
2 cups vanilla ice cream
2 large ice cubes

Dissolve jelly crystals in water. Add ice cream and ice cubes. Place in a container with a firmly fitting lid.
Shake until you can no longer hear the ice cubes. Pour into 4–6 individual dishes.
Place in the fridge for 35–40 minutes to set.

Serves 4–6

BLENDER VANILLA PUDDING

1½ cups cold milk
2 tbsp gelatine granules
1 cup boiling milk
2 eggs
½ cup sugar
⅛ tsp salt
2 tsp vanilla essence
1 cup ice cubes

Pour half a cup of the cold milk into a blender and sprinkle over the gelatine. Allow to stand until gelatine granules are moist. Add boiling milk, cover and process at low speed until gelatine dissolves (about 2 minutes).
Stop blender, add eggs, sugar, salt, vanilla essence and remaining cold milk.
Cover and process at high speed for 1 minute. Remove cover and, with blender still running, add ice cubes one at a time. Continue to process until ice has melted. Pour immediately into dishes.
Place in fridge to set (approximately 20–30 minutes).

Serves 4–6

BREAD AND BUTTER PUDDING

¼ cup sultanas
¼ cup raisins
¼ cup brandy
450 ml milk
100 ml cream
3 eggs
⅓ cup sugar
1 tsp vanilla essence
½ tsp ground nutmeg
¼ tsp ground cinnamon
100 g butter, softened
12 slices white bread

Place sultanas, raisins and brandy in a bowl and leave to soak overnight.
Preheat oven to 180°C.
Whisk together milk, cream, eggs, sugar, vanilla essence, nutmeg and cinnamon.
Butter the bread and place a layer at the bottom of a greased casserole dish, butter side up. Sprinkle with a third of the fruit mixture. Repeat layers, finishing with a layer of bread.
Pour the milk mixture over the bread. Once mixture has soaked into the bread, cover and cook for 35–40 minutes.
Serve with either custard or cream, or both.

Serves 6–8

CARROT PUDDING

1 cup finely grated carrots
½ cup sultanas
½ cup chopped dates
½ cup currants
½ cup water
½ cup brown sugar
90 g butter
½ tsp baking soda
1 egg, lightly beaten
1 cup self-raising flour
½ tsp mixed spice
1 tbsp lemon juice

Preheat oven to 190°C.
Combine carrots, dried fruit, water, sugar and butter in a saucepan.
Bring to the boil. Simmer for 5 minutes.
Remove from the heat and stir in baking soda. Cool to room
temperature.
Stir in egg, sifted flour, mixed spice and lemon juice.
Pour into a 23-cm casserole dish or divide evenly into muffin pans.
Bake for 30 minutes if using casserole dish, or 15–20 if using
muffin pans.

Serves 4–6

CUSTARD SAUCE

2 heaped tsp custard powder
2 cups milk
2 eggs
2 heaped tsp sugar

Mix custard powder with a little of the milk to make a smooth cream.
Pour into a small saucepan. Add remaining milk, eggs and sugar
and heat over a medium heat, stirring continuously until thick.
Do not boil.

Serves 4–6

CHOCOLATE SAUCE PUDDING

1 cup flour
2 tsp baking powder
½ tsp salt
½ cup sugar
4 heaped tbsp cocoa
4 tbsp melted butter
1 cup milk
1 tsp vanilla essence
2 cups brown sugar
4 heaped tbsp cocoa
2 cups boiling water

Preheat oven to 180°C.
To make pudding, sift flour, baking powder, salt, sugar and cocoa into a mixing bowl. Add butter, milk and vanilla and mix well. Pour into a deep buttered dish.
Combine brown sugar and cocoa and sprinkle over pudding. Pour over boiling water and bake for 40 minutes.

Serves 6–8

FRUIT SALAD

1 can pear quarters
1 can sliced peaches
1 banana, sliced
1 punnet strawberries, quartered
1 punnet raspberries
1 passionfruit

Pour pears and peaches into a serving bowl, including the juice.
Add all other ingredients, or any other of your favourite fruits, and
gently fold together.
Refrigerate for 30 minutes before serving.

Serves 4–6

159

LEMON PUDDING

100 g butter
1 cup caster sugar
½ cup flour
½ tsp baking powder
zest and juice of 2 lemons
2 cups milk
4 eggs, separated

Preheat oven to 160°C. Grease a 2-litre pudding dish.
Cream butter until light and fluffy. Add sugar a tablespoon at a time, stirring well between each addition.
Sift flour and baking powder and add to the creamed mixture.
In a separate bowl, place lemon zest and juice, milk and egg yolks and whisk to combine.
Fold egg yolk mix into butter, sugar and flour mix, being careful not to over-mix.
Whisk egg whites until stiff and fold them in. Spoon into the greased pudding dish.
Bake for 35–40 minutes.

Serves 4–6

PEACH AND CHERRY COBBLER

820 g can peaches and their juice
1 cup fresh or tinned cherries, stones removed
1 cup flour
3 tsp baking powder
½ tsp salt
120 g butter
½ cup milk, plus a little extra for brushing
caster sugar for dusting

Preheat oven to 200°C.
Place peaches and cherries in a deep ovenproof dish.
Sift flour, baking powder and salt. Rub in butter. Add milk gradually,
mixing to a soft dough.
Knead for a minute, then press out onto a floured surface to about
half an inch (about 1 cm) thick. Cut rounds with a floured, fluted
cutter and place, slightly overlapping, on top of fruit.
Brush with milk and dust with caster sugar.
Bake for 18–20 minutes.

Serves 4–6

PLUM JAM ROLY POLY

300 g flour
2 tsp baking powder
1 tbsp caster sugar
¼ tsp salt
zest of 1 lemon
150 g butter, cubed
120 ml milk
200 g plum jam
1 cup boiling water
1 cup white sugar

Preheat oven to 180°C.
Place all dry ingredients in a food processor. Add lemon zest and butter. Pulse until mixture resembles breadcrumbs. Place in a mixing bowl and stir in milk so mixture is soft but not sloppy.
On a floured bench, roll out dough to 20 x 30 cm. Spread the jam onto the dough. Roll up the dough like a Swiss roll. Cut into six even-sized pieces. Place in a well-greased baking dish, edge side down.
In a jug, mix boiling water and sugar to make a syrup. Gently pour hot syrup over pudding. Cover dish with foil and bake for 30 minutes, remove foil and bake for a further 15 minutes.
Serve with custard and whipped cream.

Serves 4–6

RHUBARB AND APPLE SHORTCAKE

6 large cooking apples, peeled, cored and thinly sliced
2 cups roughly chopped rhubarb
2 tbsp sugar
2 tbsp water
250 g butter
250 g sugar
2 eggs
370 g flour
2 tsp baking powder
a little milk for brushing

Combine apples and rhubarb in a saucepan. Sprinkle with sugar, add water and cook over a medium heat until apples and rhubarb are just soft. Allow to cool.
Cream butter and sugar, add eggs and mix well. Mix in sifted flour and baking powder. Cover with plastic food wrap and refrigerate for 30 minutes.
Preheat oven to 180°C.
Divide dough in half and roll into 2 circles, approximately 30 cm in diameter.
Place a sheet of dough into a greased 30-cm pie dish. Cover with apple and rhubarb mixture, then place remaining sheet of dough on top and seal the edge. Brush with milk and bake for 40–45 minutes or until cooked through.

Serves 8–10

STEAMED GOLDEN SYRUP PUDDING

80 ml golden syrup
175 g self-raising flour
75 g butter
60 g sugar
zest of 1 lemon
pinch of salt
1 egg
100 ml milk

Grease a 1-litre pudding basin and pour golden syrup into the bottom. Sieve flour into a bowl then add butter, sugar, lemon zest and salt. Rub together until mixture resembles breadcrumbs. This can also be done in a food processor.
Place egg in separate bowl and whisk until smooth, then add milk and whisk to combine.
Pour egg mix into flour mix and beat well for approximately 10 minutes. Pour mixture into the pudding basin and cover with greaseproof paper and foil. Place in a large saucepan of simmering water, cover and cook for 1½ hours.

Serves 4–6

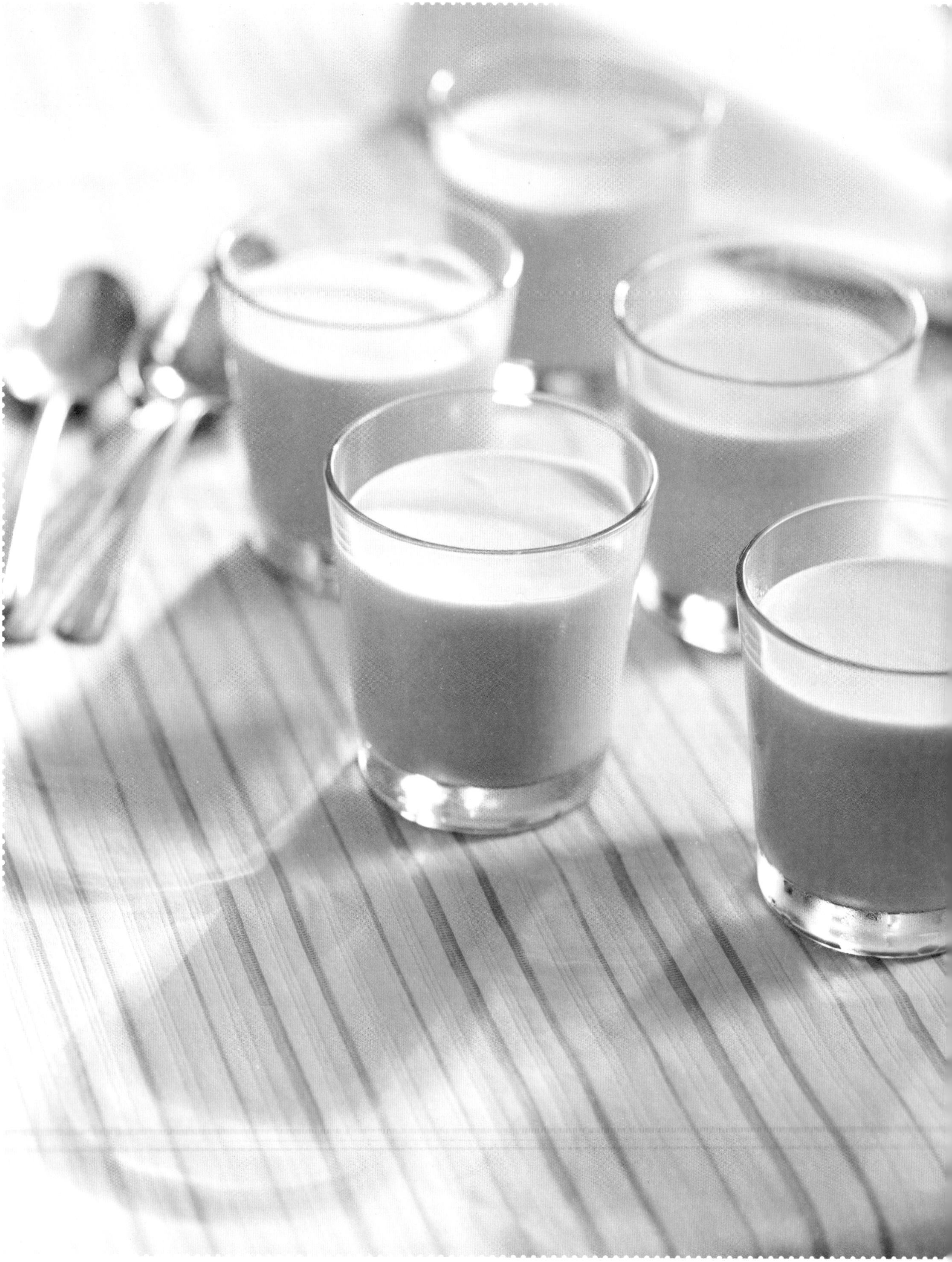

SUNSET MOUSSE

1 cup golden syrup
1 tbsp gelatine granules
1 cup cold water
4 egg yolks
2 cups cream, whipped
zest and juice of 2 lemons

Heat golden syrup to boiling point. Remove from heat.
Combine gelatine granules with cold water. Stir to dissolve and set aside.
Beat egg yolks in a bowl and stir into golden syrup very slowly.
Return to heat and stir over a low temperature until mixture thickens.
Remove pan from stove and add gelatine and water. Stir until combined, then set aside to cool.
When just about to set, lightly stir in whipped cream, lemon zest and juice.
Pour into a jelly mould, or individual ramekins. Chill to set.

Serves 4–6

PRESERVES AND SAUCES

This section of the book is in many ways my favourite, as it is about giving. Gran loved to give, whether it was through her dressmaking, cake decorating, hairdressing, flowers from her beautiful garden, or her culinary expertise. Gran gave her love freely. To give in this way is something I aspire to daily in my own life. As Gran used to say, 'It's not what you do, but how much love you put into the doing.' She had such a heart for people, and loved to share with others as much love as she could. Gran had a special cupboard where she kept all her preserves, sauces, jams and pickles. We would often venture into that cupboard when we arrived at her house, just so we could view the amazing array of jars and bottles and their contents, and speculate on what we might be given to take home. Inside each jar and bottle was a reminder of a season past: the golden glow of sun-kissed apricots, the rustic red of summer berries, and garden mint encased in jelly.

Gran and Pop would visit our family home often, and we would all wait with anticipation, wondering what delicacies would arrive with them. We would watch at the window as Pop walked up the driveway, carrying a basket of goodies covered by a crisp linen tea towel. We loved trying to feel what it was that lay beneath the covering, and would chatter with excitement as 'the unveiling' took place, revealing the delicious contents within.

PRESERVES AND SAUCES

APPLE SAUCE

4 large apples, peeled, cored and quartered
1 tbsp water
2 tbsp butter
1 tbsp sugar
1 tsp lemon juice

Place all ingredients in a saucepan and simmer until apples are soft enough to beat with a fork. Mix until smooth. Store in fridge for up to 2 weeks.

Makes approximately 1 cup

PLUM JAM

1 kg plums, stones removed
750 g sugar
1 tsp salt

Place plums in a large saucepan and cover with sugar. Refrigerate overnight.
Bring to the boil, stirring until sugar has dissolved. Continue to boil until jam sets when tested. Add salt then pour into sterilised jars.

Makes approximately 6–8 small jars

APRICOT SAUCE

1.5 kg ripe apricots, roughly chopped
400 g tomatoes, roughly chopped
450 g apples, peeled, cored and roughly chopped
3 onions, roughly chopped
5¼ cups spiced vinegar, see p. 193
3 tsp salt
10 cups sugar
3 tsp ground ginger
1 tsp ground white pepper

Place all ingredients in a large saucepan and cook for about 2 hours or until pulped. Strain through a colander and bottle.

Makes 10–12 300-ml bottles

APPLE CHUTNEY

2 kg Granny Smith apples, peeled, cored and finely diced
1 kg onions, finely diced
250 g raisins
5 cups spiced vinegar, see p. 193
1 kg sugar
500 g treacle
3 tsp salt
1 tsp cayenne pepper
2 tsp cloves

Place apples, onions and raisins in a large saucepan. Add vinegar and bring to the boil. Add remaining ingredients, stirring until sugar has dissolved. Simmer until thick, about 1 hour. Pour into sterilised jars and seal immediately.

Makes approximately 12 small jars

FAMILY MAYO

4 tbsp apple cider vinegar
1 egg
1 tsp salt
1½ tsp mustard powder
1 tbsp sugar
1 cup sunflower oil
½ cup sweetened condensed milk

Place vinegar, egg, salt, mustard powder and sugar in a blender and
blend for 30 seconds on medium speed.
Turn to full speed and drizzle in oil. Lastly pour in condensed milk.
Blend to combine.
Store in fridge for up to 1 week.

Makes 1½ cups

BOTTLED TOMATOES

1 kg ripe tomatoes

Slice a cross at the bottom of each tomato and place in a large bowl.
Pour over enough boiling water to cover all tomatoes, then leave to
stand for 5 minutes. Drain, then peel off skins.
Pack the tomatoes tightly into jars and seal.
Place a rack at the bottom of a large saucepan, then half fill with
water. Place the jar(s) on the rack, cover and bring to the boil. Steam
for 30–40 minutes depending on the size of your jar(s): 30 minutes
for a small jar, 40 minutes for a large one.

Makes 1 large jar or 2 small jars

DULCIE MAY KITCHEN

Peach Chutney

250g

PEACH CHUTNEY

2 kg peaches, stoned
2 onions, quartered
2 Granny Smith apples, cored and chopped
30 g ginger, peeled and grated
410 g can tomatoes
700 g white sugar
2¾ cups spiced vinegar, see p. 193
2 tbsp salt
2 tsp nutmeg
2 tsp cinnamon

Place peaches, onions, apples and ginger in a food processor and pulse until fine. Transfer into a large saucepan, then add remaining ingredients. Bring to the boil, then reduce heat to a simmer until thick (about 1½ hours). Stir occasionally to prevent chutney from sticking. Ladle into sterilised jars and seal.

Makes approximately 6–8 small jars

GREEN CHILLI AND CORIANDER AIOLI

2 green chillies, seeded and chopped
½ clove garlic
juice of 1 lemon
1 egg (at room temperature)
250 ml sunflower oil
8 fresh coriander leaves
salt and pepper

Place chillies, garlic, lemon juice and egg in a blender and blend for
1 minute. While blender is still running, slowly pour in oil until
mixture emulsifies. Add coriander leaves and blend for a few seconds
or until leaves are mixed through. Season with salt and pepper.

Makes approximately 1½ cups

SPICED VINEGAR

1200 ml white vinegar
2 tbsp fresh ginger, peeled and sliced
2 tbsp salt
½ tsp cayenne pepper
1 tbsp cloves
1 tbsp peppercorns
1 heaped cup sugar

Boil all ingredients together for 15 minutes, strain, then pour into
sterilised bottles and seal.

Makes approximately 4–6 300-ml bottles

PESTO

1 clove garlic
6 cups fresh basil leaves
½ cup toasted pinenuts
½ cup Parmesan, grated
2 tbsp lemon juice
dash of olive oil
salt and pepper

Blend all ingredients together in a food processor except salt and pepper until combined. Season with salt and pepper.
Store in fridge for 3–4 days.

Makes approximately 1½–2 cups

ONIONS IN CURRY SAUCE

1 cup salt
1200 ml hot water
2.5 kg peeled and sliced onions
2 tbsp flour
1 tbsp curry powder
1 tsp mustard
1 tbsp cloves
1 tbsp allspice
2 tsp turmeric
600 ml vinegar
2¾ cups brown sugar

Dissolve salt in hot water and pour over onions, then leave for
24 hours.
Drain onions and pack into sterilised jars.
Combine flour, curry powder, mustard, cloves, allspice and turmeric
to make a paste, using a little of the vinegar.
In a saucepan, boil the sugar and remaining vinegar, stirring until
sugar is dissolved. Add spice paste, stir until thick and leave to boil
for a few minutes. Pour sauce into jars over onions and seal.

Makes approximately 10 small jars

CONVERSION CHART

Fahrenheit	Centigrade	Gas Mark	Description
225°F	105°C	¼	Very cool
250°F	120°C	½	
275°F	130°C	1	Cool
300°F	150°C	2	
325°F	165°C	3	Low–moderate
350°F	180°C	4	Moderate
375°F	190°C	5	
400°F	200°C	6	Moderately hot
425°F	220°C	7	Hot
450°F	230°C	8	
475°F	240°C	9	Very hot

Liquid measurements		
½ fl. oz	15 ml	1 tbsp
1 fl. oz	30 ml	⅛ cup
2 fl. oz	60 ml	¼ cup
4 fl. oz	120 ml	½ cup
8 fl. oz	240 ml	1 cup
16 fl. oz	480 ml	1 pint

INDEX

ACKNOWLEDGEMENTS

When I self-published my first book, *Gran's Kitchen*, I was overwhelmed by the number of people who committed themselves to working alongside me, to help me realise my dream. I learnt much from the experience of compiling my first book, and I continue to learn, as I meet and work with so many new and amazing individuals. I am grateful for the many people who have encouraged me to pursue my passion of inspiring others to create food, and to share that food with heartfelt love.

Gran's Family Table is the next part of my journey. However, this book would not have been possible without the input of so many people. I would like firstly to pay tribute to my family. My sister Michelle, who cooked and styled the food for this book, is an inspiration to me. She always stayed focused on the job at hand, even with her two beautiful boys to take care of. Her energy on the days when I was required to be elsewhere was unstoppable. For this I will always be grateful.

To Mum and Dad, who took full control of Dulcie May Kitchen while I was working on the book: thank you for your commitment and belief in me, and for the energy and time you have invested in me and my dreams. This book would have been impossible without you being on board.

To my family at home, Gabby and Adam, thank you for your patience throughout this process. Life has certainly changed for us in the past few years with the opening of Dulcie May Kitchen, and the publishing of my two books. Thank you for continuing to be yourselves, in a life that has certainly changed.

To Alan Brown, who baked all the bread featured in this book. Your love of food is inspirational, and your talent phenomenal. I thank you for sharing this talent with me, and for inviting me into your home to share a meal from time to time, which always ended up being three-course extravaganzas! I am grateful for the friendship we have nurtured, and I look forward to many more long nights of food, wine and exceptional company.

To Sharon Deheer: thank you for all the lovely props you loaned me for our photo shoots, and for giving up your time to introduce us to the many places we needed to know about, in order to acquire those additional bits and pieces.

This book would not have eventuated without the support of those who had faith in me, supported me, and mentored me when I published my first book, *Gran's Kitchen*. To Geoff Blackwell: although you have not been part of the process for this project, you provided the impetus for me to continue creating books, and share my love of food with others. Your encouragement, time and expertise during the last few years has had a huge impact on my life, so thank you for being the man you are — simply inspiring. I would also like to thank Murray Brown from Books R Us. Murray, along with Carole, believed in *Gran's Kitchen* from the start, and did an outstanding job directing the sales for the New Zealand market. Thank you for taking *Gran's Kitchen* to a success I never believed possible, paving the way for me to write *Gran's Family Table*.

To my extended family who came along to our family picnic at Huia — a place where Granny spent a lot of her childhood — and to photographer Todd Eyre who captured that afternoon so beautifully on camera. To Ivan and June Booker, Leone Ward and Jim Bryson, Ashley and Heather Burrell, Eddie and Sharon Deheer, Graeme, Susan, Rhianna, Danielle and Annalise Booker, Michelle, Connor, and Elliot Burrell, and Adam and Gabby Oldfield — thank you all for sharing in this special day. It is always great to keep our family memories alive with occasions like this, and I appreciate the incredible culinary delights you all contributed.

To the many customers I have met at Dulcie May Kitchen, thank you for encouraging me to continue living my dream and for shining some of your light on my path. In return, I hope to inspire you to follow your heart and live the dreams you have imagined.

To Libby Nicholson-Moon, for your incredible writing expertise. Thank you for understanding me, and capturing my childhood memories so perfectly. You, like many of my other customers, have become more than a regular face at my store, someone I now call a friend.

To Todd Eyre, my photographer. It was wonderful to have you on this journey with me. You had the chance to meet and photograph Dulcie a few weeks before she passed away, so I know you experienced her love of family and people, and this was a huge part of why I wanted you on this project with me. Thank you for taking the time to understand what I wanted to achieve with the photography. It was a long process, with every recipe represented by a photo, but I believe we have achieved a magical result. I certainly look forward to working with you again in the future, and I know I have made a friend for life.

First a customer, then a friend, and now someone I am working with at HarperCollins — Dawn Allan. Thank you for introducing me to your team and supporting what I was doing from the start. Without your belief in me, I wouldn't be working on this project with you now.

To Alison Brook from HarperCollins. You have made it possible for me to produce an incredible book, full to overflowing with my heartfelt memories. Thank you for taking the time to understand my vision, and for being patient with deadlines.

Finally, I could not have written this book without the huge influence of my Gran, who passed away on 28 March 2009. Gran, this is for you. Thank you from the bottom of my heart, for instilling in me the drive and passion to live the life I imagined, and to share with others the love that food creates.

NATALIE OLDFIELD

ABOUT THE AUTHOR

Natalie Oldfield is the owner of award-winning store Dulcie May Kitchen in Mt Eden, Auckland. Natalie opened the doors of her now renowned store in February 2009 to coincide with the release of her first self-published book, *Gran's Kitchen*. This book went on to win the Gourmand Book Award in Europe, for best local cuisine in New Zealand. Since then, *Gran's Kitchen* has also been published in Australia and Great Britain, with Natalie adding a *Recipe Notebook* to her self-published collection.

Natalie's love for food and people meant she spent her formative years in the hospitality industry. It was during this time that her entrepreneurial endeavours led her to establish several corporate cafés and function venues, and, eventually, inspired by her grandmother, she opened her own establishment.

Published by HarperCollins New Zealand, *Gran's Family Table*, with its stunning photography and mouth-watering recipes, is Natalie's continuing tribute to her grandmother, Dulcie May Booker, who will always remain her inspiration.